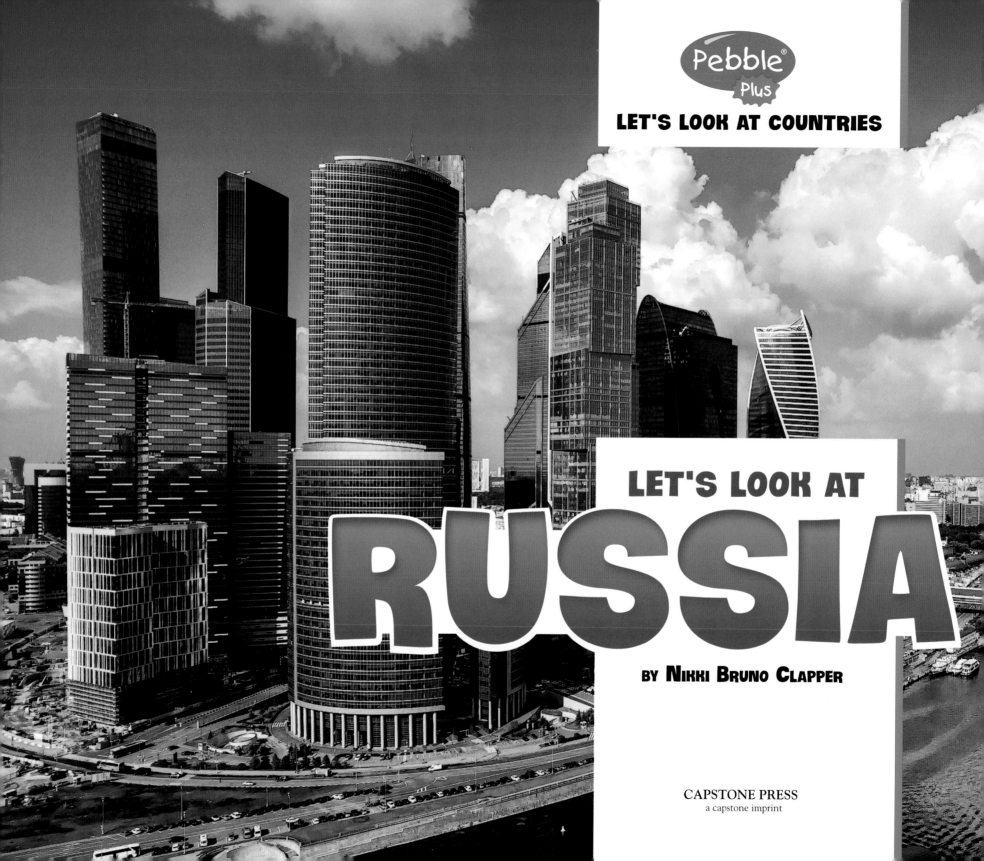

Pebble® Plus

LET'S LOOK AT COUNTRIES

LET'S LOOK AT

RUSSIA

BY NIKKI BRUNO CLAPPER

CAPSTONE PRESS
a capstone imprint

Pebble Plus is published by Capstone Press,
1710 Roe Crest Drive, North Mankato, Minnesota 56003
www.mycapstone.com

Library of Congress Cataloging-in-Publication Data
Names: Clapper, Nikki Bruno, author.
Title: Let's look at Russia / by Nikki Bruno Clapper.
Description: North Mankato, Minnesota : Pebble Plus, an imprint of
Capstone Press, 2018. | Series: Let's look at countries | Includes bibliographical
  references and index. | Audience: Ages 4-8.
Identifiers: LCCN 2017037878 (print) | LCCN 2017043283 (ebook) | ISBN
  9781515799306 (eBook PDF) | ISBN 9781515799184 (hardcover) | ISBN
  9781515799245 (pbk.)
Subjects: LCSH: Russia (Federation)--Juvenile literature.
Classification: LCC DK510.23 (ebook) | LCC DK510.23 .C58 2018 (print) |
DDC 947--dc23
LC record available at https://lccn.loc.gov/2017037878

Editorial Credits
Juliette Peters, designer; Tracy Cummins, media researcher; Laura Manthe, production specialist

Photo Credits
Dreamstime: Mengtianhan, 16-17; iStockphoto: Pro-syanov, 13; Shutterstock: Aleksandr Kutskii,
10, Boris Rezvantsev, Cover Bottom, Ekaterina Bykova, 21, EvgenySHCH, 5, Katvic, 9, KUSHELEV
IVAN, Cover Top, Martin Mecnarowski, 11, mutee meesa, 22 Top, nale, 4, NaumB, Cover Middle,
Cover Back, Nikitin Victor, 6-7, Pavel L Photo and Video, 14, Tatiana Grozetskaya, 3, Timolina, 19,
Viacheslav Lopatin, 1, 22-23, 24, vladimir salman, 15

Note to Parents and Teachers

The Let's Look at Countries set supports national curriculum standards for social studies related
to people, places, and culture. This book describes and illustrates Russia. The images support early
readers in understanding the text. The repetition of words and phrases helps early readers learn
new words. This book also introduces early readers to subject-specific vocabulary words, which are
defined in the Glossary section. Early readers may need assistance to read some words and to use
the Table of Contents, Glossary, Read More, Internet Sites, Critical Thinking Questions, and Index
sections of the book.

Printed in the United States of America.
010774S18

TABLE OF CONTENTS

Where Is Russia?

Russia is the largest country in the world. It is in Europe and Asia. Russia is almost twice as big as the United States. Its capital is Moscow.

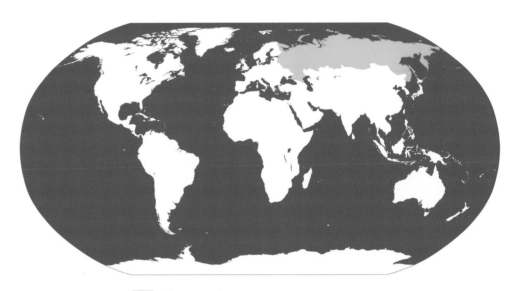

Russia

From Forest to Tundra

Forests cover half of Russia.

In the north is frozen tundra.

The Ural Mountains stretch

north to south. Russia also

has plains and marshes.

Russia has thousands of
rivers and lakes. Lake Baikal
is the world's deepest lake.
It is about 1 mile
(1.6 kilometers) deep.

In the Wild

Bears and Siberian tigers
roam Russian forests.
Snow leopards hunt
in the mountains.
Musk oxen live in the tundra.

musk oxen

Siberian tiger

People

Many groups of people

live in Russia. Most are Slavic.

Other people include Tatars,

Ukrainians, and Bashkirs.

On the Job

Many Russians build machines, cars, or ships. Others help people. They include nurses, teachers, and food servers.

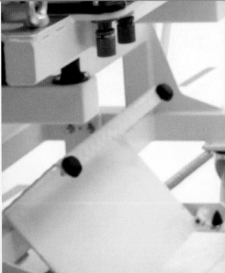

At the Ballet

Russia is famous for ballet. Many great ballet dancers are Russian. Dancers leap and spin. They perform at theaters in big cities.

At the Table

Russians eat a lot of soup, cabbage, and fish. Borscht is beet soup. It is served with sour cream.

borscht

Famous Site

The Kremlin is a group
of buildings in Moscow.

It includes churches and palaces.

Russia's president lives there.

QUICK RUSSIA FACTS

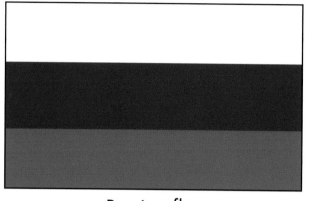

Russian flag

Name: Russian Federation

Capital: Moscow

Other major cities: St. Petersburg, Novosibirsk, Yekaterinburg

Population: 142,355,415 (July 2016 estimate)

Size: 6,592,850 square miles (17,075,400 sq km)

Language: Russian

Money: ruble

GLOSSARY

ballet—a performance that uses dance to tell a story

capital—the city in a country where the government is based

marsh—an area of wet, low land usually covered in grasses and low plants

plain—a large, flat area with few trees

president—the highest elected job in a class, business, or country

tundra—a cold area of northern Europe, Asia, and North America where trees do not grow; the ground stays frozen in the tundra for most of the year

READ MORE

Ganeri, Anita. *Russia: A Benjamin Blog and His Inquisitive Dog Guide.* Country Guides, with Benjamin Blog and His Inquisitive Dog. Chicago: Heinemann Raintree, 2015.

Moon, Walt K. *Let's Explore Russia.* Let's Explore Countries. Minneapolis: Bumba Books, Lerner Publications, 2017.

Schuetz, Kari. *Life in a Tundra.* Biomes Alive! Minneapolis: Bellwether Media, Inc., 2016.

INTERNET SITES

Use FactHound to find Internet sites related to this book.

Visit *www.facthound.com*

Just type 9781515799184 and go.

Check out projects, games and lots more at
www.capstonekids.com

CRITICAL THINKING QUESTIONS

1. What types of land does Russia have?

2. Look at the photo on page 10. What features do musk oxen have that might help them live in the cold tundra?

3. Look at the photo on page 21. Why do you think there is a wall around the Kremlin?

INDEX